HOMES

HOMES

Moheb Soliman

COFFEE HOUSE PRESS
Minneapolis
2021

Coffee House Press books are available to the trade through our primary distributor, Consortium Book Sales & Distribution, cbsd.com or (800) 283-3572. For personal orders, catalogs, or other information, write to info@coffeehousepress.org.

Coffee House Press is a nonprofit literary publishing house. Support from private foundations, corporate giving programs, government programs, and generous individuals helps make the publication of our books possible. We gratefully acknowledge their support in detail in the back of this book.

LIBRARY OF CONGRESS CATALOGING-IN-PUBLICATION DATA

Names: Soliman, Moheb, 1979– author.
Title: Homes / Moheb Soliman.
Identifiers: LCCN 2021002806 | ISBN 9781566896092 (trade paperback)
Subjects: LCGFT: Poetry.
Classification: LCC PS3619.O432564 H66 2021 | DDC 811/.6—dc23
LC record available at https://lccn.loc.gov/2021002806

PRINTED IN THE UNITED STATES OF AMERICA

28 27 26 25 24 23 22 21   1 2 3 4 5 6 7 8

HOMES

From jots at probably Tommy Thompson
Park, Toronto when this all started

Concrete rubble to Lake Ontario   *wear me down to my girders*   the lake
the half-naked lake   slipping off its jersey   started in with its cats' tongue

At Point Pelee—Leamington,
Sandusky—Cedar Point

This beach has more than two sides   more than the lake   and the parking lot
and cultivated and sandwiches farms and kiosked   aside it   and defies
properties   I've peed   behind every sorta flora   scared   away
all kinda fauna   I crossed the lines   of r&r   to bridge the banks of
main and head streets and waters   I tried myself   had myself   washed
ashore to hamlets   faceup   the whole time   my figure   a petty viaduct
only shallow beach could love   I swam each day I changed   myself inside
the Corolla   and diasporaed   footfulls of mollusky sand all over the motel
districts of Canuck Sanduskys   where in touch more   with   nature's
what   they   are   more   than   amusement or   national   park   and lark
Cedar Point and the   tip   this land does not come to   two   states   means
ends   nations   and defies commodity   recreation's and conservation's
this place   has   more   than   the   all-night   or   primitive
drive-thru and the camping   this whole time
my body held in feet   of surf   not diverting to the water   or exiting
but bridges fail all the time nothing new   bridges are being built and rebuilt
all over these lakes   adding sides to   no end   defying the accounts
of travelers   homing in   pointing out   *we came in off the water*
not really having been   out there   you come out of the water turn right
around get back in there   I'm going out to the water   never really having
left there

2

Sand mowed out in rows   dog lapping lake at Indiana   and   the   city
already game   the morning haze   in its court   what moves   lakegulls
and the day before last's news park and ride park and ride   the little lot and
water quiet and untidy   the sun checks off old   Sears Tower like a pupil high
in bright black glasses   up inside   you'd see it   this breezy pull-off
and put Michigan in the picture at the same off-balance instant   looking out
with a cloud's countenance   skimming the lake and having   horizontigo
the periphery can be so capacious when you trace it   never even seeing the
living-in-the-Loop lake rise go to work on its own   three legs   south of
itself   combing the beach for example or tempering the Wabash
Avenue runoff   with the glacial's   grooming city life to nature's
this is the height of diversity   even always seeing the lake through
the slobber

Casting myself in the man   bragging to friend or family   brag to me
motorboats coming in out the baited fog like names returning to relatives
sunset catches in their stern talk   the lake a smoldering rec hall with
one colossal rusted pickup of an ore dock towed beside   *a fish this big*
says dad   a wallop like this   punches uncle   brag   to me
no cooler a dusk since   I can't remember   pulling the truck up
reeling the boat in   *so I let the dang fish go*

I would marry you   family   just   to be   able to brag to Mrs.
sinking the sunset between the dishes   and stacking them next to the
taconite ships passing the windowsill on taco night with smoked fish   boy
dries the plasticware collects all the agates seen through the screen door the
Two Harbors skyline   of sun down on two ore docks

Where we lingered till dark   not a ship to tare between the two of us
just a ride to share   one foot   driven   into the lake   another
pensive as a passenger   and   the   last   two   asleep
under themselves like children   the tourist and work vista of Lake Superior
remember that livelihood forever   *a catch this*   lucky   hugs Courtney
brag to me brag to me   honey   baby   Robby

Lake St. Clair was a peacock, I was the pea, plump and fair   in the wild
the male are beautiful   and bare their throats like candle threads and coo
to the cooped-up who swoon and wet their   matches   as   soon   as   they   set
eyes on the wild

I was a pea and the lake was the peacock   turquoise   eyes   flush
with my chest and mmmm   mwww   mwah   pecking my shoulders in deep
and shining candor and armor   I lost myself   my clothes I wet myself   I came
I swimming   I carried my body in like a bike   I   changed   myself
in the water   paisleyed in the whorls   tell me what we do I begged

There between the burbs of Detroit and Windsor I was in the company of aqua
lified city buoy   ant Lake St. Clair and laid   in tied by water arms
and counted ten   toes   on my back drifted   like a glass fork with
three hips   against the breaks of each mouthpiece   my first time
I wanted to be sensational   in nature male is beautiful

Lake St. Clair was a peacock   not feminized or conquered   but iridescent
and masculine   I was a babe in comparison   muscles floaters   fear smell
in the wind   we mooned hotshot Ontario flicked off the thumb of Michigan
and fairly well off on the horizon   heard   tomorrow's rooster Huron

We delayed too long with the Mackinac fudge   girls stand   and   then
everywhere was booked or tons of money   But the national forest was
open land   free,   protecting itself through no hint of natural wonder
It was: Woods   The monotony astonished me   Weaving in slow, new, no view,
we soon began to understand a whole country wooded, a whole region of
higher ground,   pervasively wooded   where any clearing must have
meant something extraordinary   like water's here,   or   a   people
stayed   I saw Michigan up between the big lakes   like a boulder of moss,
a chest of tree millions   a word posted up on a few dozen stakes somewhere
on the sandy shore with a bad translation under   It   was   woods;   WOOD
Pinioned by lake beside lake beside lake, aloof and anonymous by its
tallness; forest that was young   from cutting and   square   in its   demeanor
It was only: *well, come*   We raised a flyless tent and took an unmarked
walk and got lost within minutes   We deliberated about direction,   tacked
left and right and ovaled and ovaled and found our way back somehow by dark
panicked with relief I was glad we got lost Glad to know the forest was that
insoluble   and that I was indeed that much at whim, not inured to ceaseless
calculating, but good and helpless   Don't need to worry about seeking, like
the preternatural, civilization; it's imminent So what remains   to   be
found? is   the last line of the woods—just before you see the car and
camp   so   menacing   but   looking   back—is   always
retreating

Algae break   water   webs of puce   the shoreline   lipstick left by
the lake on lovesick miles of napkin good-bye   Fudgies   snap your towels
of assy sand   make the kids chase down   the wrappers   I'll replant their
gutted hawthorn and piss off   the   beach   fire   from   the   driftwood
it's time we got back to work   consummate vacation   fuck the lake
no love   to   salvage   memories of   drinking each other completely
empty of their taste   better to forget the acrid pics of summers luxuriating
with anything precious fenced   the   lifestyle   we   desired   here
the zoos of microenvironments   the patios crawling out of the mudflats with
the frogbit floating in impenetrable mats   the glassy pole dance of dusk
slick stage left   just hold your liquor and keep down the   zebra mussel-
sucking noise   when the speckled black other shoe drops just look   away
vacate the promises

It was a port that sank   not a freighter   or steamer   or one of
Perry's fleet   but a whole port, for sailboats—not leisure but pelt-era-
maritime's latest gallivanting technology; fettering the interior with mettled
whites   It was a point on the way that LaSalle anointed with French flowers
-de-lis and Father Hennepin with him in semen and Tonty in shale-sparks with
his steel claw aground   It blossomed into a port city   on the shallowest lake
of the whole unmarshaled region   Some spot in the marshes before
Leamington and beyond Ports Dover and Stanley   Personally I
believe it was Rondeau   I met a regiment of memory there
What it was   being foreigns and braves and genuinely gods-fearing and raising
a palisade and wheat and fermenting   a trade zone—that dried up—
that flooded next spring   The marine life leave some artifacts untouched
on the lake bed some conjecture; some dive; a book reports; the canon
Maps were found   with drawings of Marquette's of   the horseshoe of
Niagara less crumbled and calculated the distance to the port's crude first
European wigwams, with arrowed   hearts in the parchment's margins
Zealots' destinations; speciously-barked-up   whole woods   of ash and maple
abandoned when the faith didn't take   It's murky, what happened   What
lost, what left   the wives   kids   orphans   chattel   missions   crosses
X'ed into land escapes

Pasty in Ontonagon that faces away from
Keweenaw Peninsula nearby, will skip

Mining   they tell you   your   experience   days of   yore
but what if you're like dunes that powerlessly cover and move and short-billed
sandpipers are your nearest-by mentors   and you want to be another thing
altogether let alone   person   how much grainy plot to dump water on
and pack and dig   there's no well you fell down   you're not desert
or lake people   pack   your   belonging   in   white   handkerchief
you're going to that big blue   Corolla in the sky

I remember Keweenaw   we took a trolley down inside
the hillside   we were a couple then of sightseers   we saw the painstaking
machines and underground diagrams   in loaned-out hard hats and company
jackets we hugged the wet chambers miming the echoes   a couple of names
were etched in the copper   and that was it   and that was the finest the
oldest time there ever was   met you at Sudbury let you go at Green Bay
tested the water and industry in-between   no   end   to—
cover   and move on   forever duned

Ore of mine   grouse may brood and rain pat sand   and   grasses   ask   us
blasters-through to sit a min   before their world   blows   over   mine of ore
for some   for some it's sand all the way down   some show a hole where
some's mouths are stuffed with gold

After emptying freebie farm stand (criminal)   Hamlin Beach park   local
Pakistani folks merry   at a shabby wedding   party 40s   WPA shelter too close
to shore   built by the dads of older amblers-by   harboring the stone-
faced nature behind it all   where you start at something   like   a   possum
or a raccoon   unsure what difference there is   between us   unwilling
to drown the American within us   unable to let her   swim away   *Joyce
I'm coming*   a dachshund barks   *wait   you need help*

It's never dark enough for anyone not to see you   looking on   showing your
teeth to   show you're smiling   rubbing your baby browns under your
robber mask fit   in lighter-light   there was a full pack of menthols too
you keep everything   you get even after it's spoiled the   cukes
and pears   beefsteaks   peaches   Silver Queen corn   a country dream
forever   holding your peas   from you

The keystone robbed from the archway   the tip of the pyramid clipped
wet dollar in the stall   if you were a mother you'd understand   *Wait JOYCE do
NOT touch that man*

My phone calls all birds with its barbaric app and all can hear and who'll be laughing when a jay and a duck are talking to me and my company? my company but the guys'll love me and my yearning power and viral if I steer a moose viral can do a lot of good in our time to save a pile of trees and pileated woodpeckers of the continent of controlled burning and healing and the opening deepening scarring troubles of our time my heart cries out my butt pocket under the treetops of the wood   while   they   still   are
world
come to me as you would
your young calling
guys
wait with me
for a time

a short life such as this is fre

quented by bugs and leaves

this is a
a sweet little life
one on the wrong side
of the tracks from strife

where wildlife is
fixed
where the wild life
is a fix
of a strange light

bright but gray like today's
bright but gray like Today is

how's it fair
how's it fair
weather only
holds me together

I don't know these streets
I don't know these streets

I always see this park
I always see this park

I don't know this part
of me

is there love
a love
that is

unhuman

that's what we'll have some of

In Ontario but far from Superior or
these missed parts

You do not arrive
The place arrives
You are alive
We are alive
Wait on the risers by the shoreline
The place arrives
Places arrive
and start the fires
where there is any shot at life

Lake of the Clouds in a boat bow
finding Superior through the Carp's mouth
Porcupine Mountains in a ship stern
See me now
See me now
set to burn their hemlocks and maples

Madeline Island swimming in
to red cliffs since before reservations
Tom's Burned Down Cafe treading water
I am alive
I am alive
serves as fodder for annexed places

Sault Ste. Marie twins test boundaries
crossing the rapids of the St. Marys
Locks knee-deep in the terrain and name
Come to me
Come to me
fan the flames of their emigrations

The place arrives
Places arrive
Fabled excess of the sum of parts

Collect and gather
Not discrete no idea
Not as creatures ghosts the weather a cordless power
It is not alive
They are not alive
A clap reversed
Big bang land
Bound down boardwalks like fire
escapes
There you strand
waving your arms
But you are alive
The place arrives
shooting flares into the night
You are on fire

Please be real, beach   Please be real, sand And have been here   before the
men's room   and women's room And geese, please   keep   landing   and
more keep appearing, Vs   It's   chilly   but   I   haven't   got   other   pullovers
The clouds parka like the car   and I'll sleep in one   under the other
Take a little longer   look but   don't   touch and   go   Need to have to
have no communing for community   A parallax for this silent treatment
What all in place,   still runs   So   sun: settle,
chick; fluff your down all slowly   And moon   please   have no man
no tattoos   neither dangle talismans nor snake mnemonic
devices to fake a livelihood with the lake   Have no back   but   please
don't turn it   You're body   Your nobody mark   Make that blanched spot on
the wake that seiche that sloshes   the Lakes
They're one   Their one signature their bob   Their bob but as
indiscrete as lava   This lava   from   glaciers
to water   this beach—Erie   How   always   up   in   arms   and
temperamental   Continually crawling from its bed to rest within eyeshot and
abreast of cities like a cradle put shyly to the test by its little member as it
refuses   pleas   Wet my ear   Stir up memories of before marinas,
lake, when you were so unreal   You're so urban   rural   suburban
Come down to Westerville, OH be as close as you could get   to natural   like
myself be   exurban   Be no artist See no art just   be real
Dancers let me have this one;   let me alone   pause   I forget no steps;
please   let's leave the lake with the geese   It makes short work of
our audience   Please be real beach and please be real sand
And have been   from here   before men and women and all Corollas
that like horizons   spark out from   a far   parking   spot
Tonight I'll stop here lost at lake and my legs grow long and shallow shadows
into its dark wet sweeps   But please   stay at bay car stay   at bay   goose stars
please, outlive me

Looks like 7:50:47   this little flock striking out   like   hands   across   a
vapid face   like it's 8:02:58   noon dozens of teens slap each other
off pylons into a placid face   breaking out in   one   piece   like   a
windshield   nothing to see here officer   arrest the day   that   all   life
about-faces   and by night tosses   like keys   into the faceless body by
all quays   just out of grasp   of recognition   stuck   in the face
of oblivion   with needles   with safety pin   of danger   with
piercings   of failure   the man in   the   sun   sick   of starting the car
with a penknife every day   without a place to stick it ever   or the bottom
of the lake   a   threat   a   promise   visage

Three of us waiting for wind   her sailboat still as the morning bar
veranda   a day for harbor-dredging   not even peanut skins quivered
we wanted her to take us out in her islandry history—it was me you and last
night's Mack we met   at the Burned Down   stars shot through the
tarp roof   on-the-house   shots and microwave pizzas

Her ponytail that stood   at the edge of a ginger candle   jogger's hips in jeans
but ready   with a thin scarf around her freckled back in bathing suit
earlier at the toast-and-jam she took us to   our waiting waxing into full
relaxing   her garish humor after a tantrum   it   all
akined her to you   someone you could be   a pal
to kiss   in the empty cemetery   she showed us everything

The locals' beach past the ferry landing   we   were   lost   but   for
good   family-album-flipping aimless   I tossed you peas out in the surf
something caught   something sailed out   I felt a couple surface ripples deepen
a common otter in you both chuck like a stone   the shell break
but we never make it out

Made like ice and skid   addled by a familiar inertia   so   light   and
slow and hopeful on the road   made of frozen-over lake   plowed out past the
seasonal ferry   a   couple   miles   of   ice   exposed   to   thicken
in a sea of snow and lined with last year's Christmas trees   happy new one
islanders   next time I bring a pooch   in a hatchback   he goes where the
boy goes where his mom is   every other week   I like to take us coasting
like an escaped puck   far adrift yet only one way to go   onto the ice road
floating like the tiniest island   knees   at   the   wheel   to   write   this
fed the words by the piping lake   mufflered in a quilt of snowpack
the day a pacifier   getting warmer   warmer   warmer   mmm
made it   Madeline   shut me up   in someone's summer house
with this family till the trees sink   it could be the last time a road
liquifies into environment   a road skates off into history   year-round
ferry   terminal I mean   hey   who needs to drive out on a great big
lake see some ice caves for the last time   yawning at the rise of Wisconsin
since it last felt the polar   similar   burden of its namesake   glacier

Looking at the Genesee from so far out on pier it
must be lake now but brown and frothy still

a 12-pack of Genny is about the river   it can't be made of   they   must've
used to   can it?   drink it bathe their beer   guts in it
hot Rochester weeks   you take it down to the lake under cover   of double
walled water   bottles and two-ply   wharves   instead of a lifeguard
a chiseled notice   No Dogs No Glass Swim at Your Own Risk drink at your
own you don't have to go home   but you can't live here   well you can I

have got a growler in me   a happy pit   a Sam Patch   leapt chasms for a living
Niagara   Genesee   his motto   *some things can be done*
as well as others   you can frame a house   build a flower bed well   I
can jump a falls breathe the froth   or can I   or is it   if some things
can't be won   a whole mess of others can   just take it   one   step   at
a dive now   make do set your sights   on   whatever's at the corner
store will have to do

It all just strikes me   nothing pierces me   stony point   picture-perfect
the moment's shot   a flash goes off   though I feel the impact   my eyes
were shut nothing enters   captured in ton honeymoons   nothing misses me

The corrosion at Niagara   the plaque of pilgrims on the railings   a thick coat
of enterprise on the back of sublimity   the traffic of all that   driving crashing
water   seven hundred   and fifty   thousand   gallons per second   half
siphoned   for three million horsepower   the eroding   horseshoe
mist trampling the airways   can't get a breath in   locked in the prism
monetized sterilized two thousand   quarters   per   Tower Optical
binocular machine   then emptied   the land and taken scaped and for
granted   the sacrifice Olmsteded at every vista

To Goat Island   to the Bridal Veil   dream   Anniversary   Capital
die   dreaming   unfold the blankets strollers pamphlets complimentary
ponchos with Velcro sandals   callousness   rain down with the selfie sticks
beat down with the sun   bows for the polarized   locals foreigners   lenses
see through it all   peerless   sight   you can put baby's head   through a
face-hole board painting   of a man going over the falls   and never make it
to the wax museum across the Rainbow Bridge   tepid   life
give me your barrel   send me over   shoot me

Somebody sees us here   conjured us, in a nuclear canoe, looking behind ourself
and smiling   at where we've come   and holding it   hold it
got us   someone pictured us   crowded in a khaki rainbow   bent over a sunset
post   the moment saved   for the moment   safe   just hold it   holding it

They captured us   frogs   butterflies   wildflowers   micro
-creameries -breweries -habitats dear   and far in the rearview
but also square in our headlights   re-creation   for   recreation   for
they had to restore the nature to remaster the soundtrack to our summered
future or we die   groping in VR video at the synthesized bells of a crosswalk
for our stroller   where is she
and a set of glinting turtles   before they scroll off   into the   surf

They projected many here   posing   prone   big to small   on a living log then
shot and chopped together into a humus-colored film for us to float in   hold it
then hold it   now hold it   all our life   Life   so babyish   in   our   one
shared lipless two-hand   wiping water off the face of the planet

Last one   here we go   look at me   one more   era   smile   now glint
glimmer for a second   recreate   now re-create   for a second time
a picture then   picture now   now picture then   picture   then
now picture now   then picture then   picture us

It was the Lakes' Atlantis   Hosting ocean liners and batteaux alike   Where "beaver jam" soared and sank in the lifetime of one kit   And   First   Nations folks married Native Americans in a reverse nod to settlers' slowly muddying blood   Metropolitans   drinking every night   Shingling roofs through late afternoon lake monsoons   Gutters were reinvented   A theater company flourished   after appropriating, like boarding schools, and Jesuit schools, the Indigenous Arts   There was a moratorium on debates about polygamy, and canals   Sophisticated pollution laid out neighborhoods and spurred movements that bled into derelict rants   of even animals' rights; some thought of space even   at the expense of tangible exploration up a thousand creeks   In 2000   its old museum was excavated and piecemeal shipped to a museum   somewhere near present-day Irondequoit Bay by a replica mighty Iroquois village first torched late 1883 And again summer school 2003   by teen brothers related unknowingly to Tecumseh   who retroactively passed their American History for so poignantly repeating it   You can step in the same shit twice, the same ruin   the same grand gateway to the West   For   the   next   of countless times lost

23

The other Gary   single Gary   with the yellow truck   the one that paints
landscapes   the empty lot   walks two collies Gary   that works in Chicago
from home Gary   hybrid   uncle   ageless Gary   Nick and Dan Gary (you know
Nick and Dan) if they knew Gary   surfing Gary volunteer Gary tan veggie
photogenic Gary   gregarious Gary   white Gary okay   yeah I went there
let's go there   to   Gary Miller Gary   huddled in the dunes   by Gary Gary
poor Gary

Upscale Carp Center   *Jacks n Five Tonite*   on   Palace   marquee
It's a Child's World   next to   Casket   Showroom
on boarded-up store   downtown   in black: *If it takes a village   to raise
a child.......a clean village*   red underline   *does it*   in red: *better*

The Turning Point   past the freight lines   along front yards   near miraculous
Indiana Dunes National Lakeshore

At the courthouse   by the convention center   and   the   train   stop
The   People   of   Gary   Weclome [sic] *You*

Thunder and other bays running into one

Laptopped it   since December   keen   bay   now finally Thunder
Bay landing   stout blocky jetties   gleaming stock of water   looking back
up   Shoreline Motor Hotel   see   my   future   writing   her   mysterious
notes on the balcony   instead of missing me down here   to gaze past a couple
weeks' worth of wide open bays for us   that run   together   into
one   big bay in memory   at the end there's an airport to go   plant trees
for money in her future   honey's province   doesn't know him yet but
it's likely   we're halfway around the biggest lake   we haven't even started
we'll live together still   don't know that yet but   don't want our reading done
no charts for us nothing magic   about   our   thing   just   earthy   eye-
watering   if we married   out on the horizon   on a ship who's to say
maybe we did and we can't find it now   lotta   writing   to sift   through
lotta pictures to delete already   on one of two plush pert beds   the spoils
later in each other's laps   devices brochures hands   takeout   remote   very
much   a bounty   means some things get to go to dogs

Do   I   have   to   make   myself   known   with   every   step?
the world's littered and loud   with ex
beauty   do I have to stay?   put   where   somebody may find me
am I that lost   can't they look   .

How   can   I   have   sense   enough   for   perspective?   with   eyes
not at the sides of my face I'm human? I've   raked all the brightness
into a blind spot   rolled   in   the   back   of   my   head   where   never   mind   is
I'll remember these maple leaves all   succored   by pine trees

It's Thanksgiving in October and how unsavory   half Ontario, Huron,
Erie, Superior   and how unseasonable here on Michigan
the wind tugs a second   time and the shuck falls a trickle   a dry run from
my   cowlick   scraping   my   scarred   cheek   to   where   my   empty   chest
pocket is   do I have to wear flannel even sheets sleeping naked when—*do I*
/ have to / wear flannel / when sleeping even / for fuck's sake /
to be accepted   excuse me   oh   to   be   naturalized
into the country   the woods and water
I would do anything   I belong nowhere

I bought these Gander brand new leather boots high-neck and warm and remind
me of someone and waterproof and elegant and hunting and keep in any scent
of my aliveness so no creature can know of me whenever I visit   them   but
how   it's been so utterly   mild   so   blue   this life here   it's a
shame   not to wear them   I'll   go   out   walking
                                    I'll go down walking

                                    I came in walking
                                    I fell I hit the ground
                                    walking

26

As far as the eye can axel
there's a long long ridge
an hour's drive
past it's Lake Michigan
feels like it's right over it
long long lake wide enough
to convince the end
of the continent
calm enough
to betray that
someplace
is at the giving end
of endless waves
at the receiving end
of a tier so glass
you could almost end up
wandering across
Lake Michigan today
after surviving
the coarse brush day's
walk getting there
You could be as far
as it is large
and still
you sense it
its—not shadow—not
reach—but in the middle
of the lake's as if
circumspection
so deeply held
because it couldn't
possibly care
about you at all
ETA
lighthouse on

hospitality
be damned
so helplessly unwelcoming
a body
without embrace
but helpless
to hold anyway
feet in its face
helpless to stay
where it is
giant thing
imagine that
beyond the ridge
water dead yet
so incessantly fed
it could satisfy a bottomless

Gimme a lakefront suite you can't afford the lakefront suite gimme a basement then with the lake out the window cut in the ceiling drop it's called a garden room you can't afford the garden room flooded with the lake light lakefront carriage house lakefront cabin shack RV set out to pasture by the lakefront yurts you can't afford that a lake-view spot at least up the hill some you can't afford the hill can't afford the lake without some family land to build on convert a barn you can't convert a barn if your life hung on a rafter in it like cured by smoking what's the catch here can I get a window booth I'll have the walleye you can't afford the walleye the chowder then with the dregs of walleye which way's the lighthouse is there a local road is there a pull-off to touch a beach at least and sit in setting sun somewhere and watch a plank of water drifting out of reach warped down the center rife with rot and golden splinters good for nothing but contemplation that's what you pay for I'll go for broke for catch the harbour boat tour fifteen dollar drinks and truffle popcorn blowing out of reach call my parents sister her Miguel my baby niece she doesn't speak and gasps instead of laughs grabs my phony face lit with golden hour bitters I front like I got a sweet deal on a lake-accessible place the wheelchair room in the hotel short jog past a castle over ten CN rail lines swear from there can hear the lake swear

Perfect so you found the beach where Latinx and SWANA   birthdays
go Saturdays to barbeque their own style Chicago dogs   and beer's allowed
so aren't selling   at the rip-off stand   where the riprap starts
protecting the waterfronts of Winnetka mansions perfect   and there's only two
factories in sight perfect   some of them gotta work there   carpool or bus
some are us   a family of bikes   piled   like   briquettes
hiss to the touch in the heat   the Coke machine choked with Sacagawea
dollars and waters   out of order   the lake is fresh   if you wanna filter it
for dead fish   dead pixels in the sand   cry-colored puddles in the change room
there is no   place   like home
everywhere   we are   foreign

The road closed winters, the Porkies

Lake of the Clouds in a boundless hurry   bouncing through storm
animus with brights   chasing   that   never-to-be-seen
porcupine   featured   in the mountains   of magazines
growing in the back seat   window stuck open

the lake keeping coming in   from the sleet   to shore
from its own welts   for shelter   not possible
go back   where you   came   from
to stay   where you   not from

Home   of *Beautiful   Joe*   —the—abused dog   first
Canadian book to sell a million copies   by a humanitarian woman who
set it in Maine   under the pseudonym of a man to   win   an   American
Humane Society lit award true story   immortalized   for   all   Canadians   but
what of their national identity   whatever   "they"   is   up   on   some
lukewarm flea-bitten bay   brows knit and sticky as maple and star-crossed
flags on the main drag where they still Rollerblade   tan outdoors   little
jail looking out on two bays   and a downtown square   neat as a guest
bathroom painting   kids a quarter-mile out in dazzling sprinkling lawns just
about inside the lake   dads within shouting distance   embroidering lures
into their fishing bonnets   the   women gut   perch   so   aquatidian

I see an opening here   I'd spare no dog   be Meaford's new beloved mutt
walker   make my whole foreign clan come visit me   commit tourism
our own homegrown Egyptian brand   shirk local economies   shoot every
landmark   claim every cube owed of motel ice   where   we're   from
pet care hiking wilderness animal   rights   bit ridiculous   my dad's
dead black Lab when he was a kid   he dug up   a family property near
the Nile   cleaned and polished the skull   did his English exercises by it
still boxed in Alexandria storage somewhere   true story   he recounted at a
KOA on the way to Anchorage   the RV folding out into Costco baguettes
and pyramids of cold cut tubs   but suffered we no dog
out to stretch its legs   a little nibble   and we cuddle   dog-eat-dog on an
ancestral scale   we   more   mercenary   we   than   provident   wherever
"we" belongs

Homesick   to grow   up up here   where is the   password at
newest building's the   library   all   computers   don't need a card
need an email   need a buried pic   need rain gear   kids run the town summer
line the gummy streets askew to lake-views along the World's Most Famous Hot
Dog Shop on the World's Most Historic Port this historic   port that   sick of it
need an address to be   mailed at   need my   rain gear
need a homeboy   need a Hangout   some sun no more screen burn
order rain gear   really really   really need some rain gear

Tettegouche where another river though it's water   falls still has a mouth
on the lake   rivers have mouths   lakes have bodies   the math after
where towns straddle   past Grand Portage,   Grand Marais
how many mouths have to throw up into lake   before it all goes sour
is there no end   the   baby   can   go   with   the   bathwater
and wade happily into the expanse?   their not-stingy binging always purging
gorgeous   kiss going straight   to the hips   of the lake   mouths; bodies
alongside,   World's Best Donuts holds down the waterfront till frost
cakes the lips of the Baptism and lines the waist of Superior where proprietors
stay and hibernate   people   rivers   lakes   all   have   beds
the formers' dug   the latters' dredged   the formers lie in   pass away
the latters soak the sheets   eat   away   the   living   edge

Shallow Awenda so beautiful Bay it makes me naked and no eyes look away I
wanted to   come to the lakeshore   to be with things moving in no
human way   rock horse sucked into   waves   that draw your feet
like erasers   wash the sun's rake against the lake's   floor hard honey
licking my knee   I think of you   licking your knee   of   you
you're joining me soon Pippi I'm so happy   getting June out and swimming up
shivering wet and drying out   overlaying the gloss of the rock with a buzzy nap
and sopping in its flanks of moss half the flapping Great-Lakes-states map
folding water over itself   my eligibility   judging myself   lopping off
tit and tongue   being a tan man   to share the bay with I
tremble to   be surrounded by moving things that talk in no way but
move to talk to move to talk   the trees lean brush handles   the lake
unmanageable hair nesting bird dreams birds dream of fish dinners and   water
in their noses water makes a bed lies in and spills over   without a word verging
on the perfect   with a grain of salt   the shore drags in my dun boulder
I dig my heels in and it brays   the water spits mimetically in waves the sand
ensconces the ripples at bottom   the template of a coliseum my touch
encounters as it effaces   I feel I will   fight an obscure peace awhile
a love that's unhuman   you started to show me how
to live so abandonedly   like a little deity at play   bashing the sun into Georgian

Its absence holds me quiet   and I don't need to go back or forth or to   hello
blues sky   hi lands   of   drizzle   where   I'll   squelch
reviving some place   time   using it   to keep your life   open
to nothingness   the hollow reeds   in the still   years   making no music
and lucky   to meet a creature that makes   no noise   in shuttering the   fields
Lucky   for   a   goose   to   walk   down   the way
kicking pebbles toward me gently   how close will it get? before flying
above me   or will it walk   right past me   and never look back   trust me

At light in Fair Haven in Fair Haven
State Park at dark

FH   driving in I hear that music   box the kids dodge across and every ice
cream   truck   twist   cone   comes   back
to me now   sublime   and cherry   and all the towns are instantly the same
few I knew   the band   stands the thrift stores the visitor centers
the poor the fenceless sandy yards swept weekends   all   around   this
blown-out region   existing everywhere at once   I missed it all so bad
before I even had recognized it   When   you   have   a   boat   you   know
boaters   they know you   if you don't   dusk is a lonely shift of shops closing
to say I've seen it all a hundred times   I've seen hundreds of some things
didn't write them down but   not whittled down   sharpened   less words but
not shut up   inside   you   find it at the next place   before the dark
gets too dark   FHSP
your hair's been cut   by   two   mirrors   in the beach town half laundromat
half barber shop and your nape is clean and a palm you didn't know you had
sees breezes   it's that beautiful of a night tonight   grateful the day is over
I could turn in   myself   if I could if   there's a bounty for the placeless
wonder if there's such a night swim so nice out there ever again like tonight's
it feels like the end of my body   tingling like a screen   porch with internet
looking for something to look up real intoxicating and dripping with brilliant
facts that will light up the night oh   that's the first thought of home since   oh
a neck   of swans just flew right over me   trumpeting   change   this winter
will be like   the feel of water in your ear   like   you   been   told   something
and the idea's finally now   cooling   trickling   see   what you'll   do   is

There   were towns   and beaches   spooning   there was longing
and belonging   and long piers re   their in-between   there was sunset
scoops of peach high and as wide smeared on the chins of breakwaters bibbed
in seaweed   Dave dove in   where   it   was   clear
I drifted in the pierced fisherman and sons' thin Spanish   sank my spitting
image onto pylons crimsoned slow below   there was perfectly lone friendship
                                    there was a glinting shopping cart there
                                    glided in the deep   with no passenger
                                                                          door
                                                                    to knock on

Another Lakeshore Dr, Lakeshore Rd

House looking for home
free me from freedom
pity me
take my house
inside your house
my roof
your rules
Knock before entering
No suits in the pool
we can live under two
invade my distance
with your privacy
put
me up
up with me
my uninhibited
dwelling
dawdling
in the shadow lawns of homes
circling the maelstrom
bring me your power
put me in my place
your place
own me forever
land on my life
still me

You make hummingbird cake with pineapple I remember You ring each other's fingers in the batter, it's a big one Big family; lake cottage has the heart's pick of big pans, big bowls Two divorced sisters, two never married, all four brought their girls up Four bunks in the loft, four bedrooms on the first floor like four square rowboats with shingled interiors, one tent by the dock, and grampa brought his camper up Dinner will be buffet style There's not a table big enough or a room big enough for a table big enough to seat everybody Dessert will be buffet style They can take it out on the deck if they wanna, Martha, says grandma with the chimes bleating against the hummingbird feeders You cook couscous and mix molasses and add a dusting of corn flour You always hold your breath while they're eating They come alone but together like relay runners, they know when you're watching, pretending like you're carving names in the Muskoka chairs They come when the girls' girls are safely out of the way way out in the water during naps on egg timers for the old-timers—who; they make the meat, you make the sweet stuff for the feeders sweep the family off its feet Everyone is humming; thank you for having me; your heart'd explode from so much harmony Ring the big dinner bell draw the well dry the eyes call the goose done Can't ever remember what the icing is made of This time of year strangely it's always a slew of their bakers' dozen birthdays

Hey man wanna buy a parking pass? / A coupon for the Queen Cruise ma'am / Who's getting high on the fitness trail / and stumbling through the lumber yard / Industrious waste of Parry Sound / Tourists getaway / while you can / Making grands off thirty thousand islands / Yacht club men pull up their khaki shorts / Daughters yank their cutoffs down / Holding hands in the harbor / of their legs / Timber shorn lathed and limber / by the smelted bed of the Seguin River / Used to be a mill here / Would go for firewood now if it were still standing dry / Making grands off thirty thousand islands / Outta rain / That poor / Library closed for summer / More baggage than a Greyhound / Peering into kitchen windows like a lone pie / full of holes and currants / Seguin Bridge's hydro-currents / addicts hookers middle schoolers / Making deals by the Seguin River / The pills the tits the fossil's real / Swearing by their mothers' lives / and stumbling through the fitness trail / And getting high by the lumber yard / Making grands off thirty thousand islands / So the story goes like any other lake-and-river town / Huron-Seguin-Parry Sound / Making grands off the Thirty Thousand Islands

Driving north from Columbus back to shore, a
nondescript northwestern inlet of Lake Erie

Here come the copses of southern trees / Driving north with all the heat /
The west getting wetter every year / Settled by stands from the east tell me
*Put down your roots like you know 'em own 'em wherever home is Moheb lay
down your full head of leaves or losing needles as is dig up your flowerless bed
and move*

There go the elms to ashes galore / In fungus fires emerald borers / From city
bends to river corners / Down with trees up with borders tell me *Put down your
roots like you know 'em own 'em wherever home is Moheb lay down your fool
head in passport pictures visas as is dig up your birth certificate and move*

*Man the island move / Fauna flora move move / Trunks in the water move /
Rock wave sand bed move move move move / Abandon the island move /
Dump storage move move / Trunks in the water move / Backpack pillow backseat bed
move move move move*

There are no titles here / forms deeds / good or spectacular / all is common /
place property history knowledge / all is equal / unceremoniousness /
and undeserved / there are no rights / wrongs here rules / it is permanent /
transgression / stomping on feet walking / in others' shoes loving / to death /
sorry man / excuse me love / there are only apologies / for all that's passed /
and all that will never come to / no inheritance / legacy / no / lease on life /
grave marker / plot no / summary / no / address / only squatters have place /
names Kingston, Marquette / Parry, Owen Sound Mo / Hamilton, Ashland /
Windsor Mo name's Schreiber / Mo Gary Mo / it's Sheboygan, Pentwater /
Blind River Mo Mackinaw, Tawas, Rogers, Grindstone City Mo name of / title if
/ homes

1 / The continent, with age, spots   I saw it from a hem-hole, bellicose
crosses, lace, baby's breath, sickly   paisley   But I'm in the heart of it now
We've been here three decades   a thin film   Orangish fuzz, mold,
knuckles, jacks, Dodges, the few great uncles   grandma off the ferry   on
the freeway   a thin film across the country   We brought them to live with
us   among the cowboys   and buckeyes   badgers and   wolverines
fighting Irish and Protestants   To cook and clean and night and day   care
To be the dogs that feed us all   We   brought   them   here   to   die   for   us
To be our first graves here   This   continent,   with   stones,   spots
Now ours are among them   Wasp nest ash, Indian monuments   Muslims
like they feared back in the home country   Plots   finally   coming   to
fruition   Plastic little blue roses   in   snow   like they've never seen in
Cairo

2 / I love my country   I'm thinking of cowboys   after tail, after pain
driving and drinking   I'm thinking   of a muraled pickup pulling horses
to a distant championship across the border   sun spilling on a passport
in   the   passenger   seat   like   a   pale   cool   golden   beer   spreading   in
over the prairies, like a Molson Canadian   Thinking of being a cowboy,
I think of being Canadian   Other   guys,   loving   countries
I'm a bad guy too   settler   immigrant, supposed to say   I hate my
country   I like those drives where there's nowhere to go   on   the
radio but twang and drawl and Jesus—I love my country   I'd   go   to   a
baseball game in a small town, sure   and   charge   the   mound   and stomp my
dead and cheer a lot and throw my little brat   my brat up in the air   I hate
my   mustard   love   me   my   ketchup   I'm   a   left-hander   that's   my   difference
That's how I write and drink punch and feed   myself senseless   That's
why we came here   That's how I die   double-fisting   Wendy's
wearing my seat belt   Hate my state, love me   my
continent

Detour into subdevelopments
like m&d's new Bluebird Dr

home frame stalled in the exurbs   deer stray in the living room   before
the track lights and double-paned   there was a window there   a shudder
of the habitat   in the neighborhood   a fawn put down a deposit rashly in the
sun through sawed beams   in the place of the fireplace   new antlers
tore through cloudy plastic to outdoors   where carpets go hooves dug   in the
gravel heap a cul-de-sac   of driveways and in the street   names   wilderness
don't leave don't move   deer

always a host in the trespass   at the open house   at the doorless home
a boulder   unearthed purposed for decor   the spools of yards of
sod for years to come   where   does   lay   worn-in welcomes
where creek otter trace   meadow robin drive   quail court fox way
rabbit view   cricket place pine glen bluff   eagle   run   don't come
don't stay deer

                              There's a vacancy in the bush
vacancy   where something lived
it's acute   little death   quills everywhere   dabbed in black blood   finally
they're tarring Lakeshore   writing thickets   off   the   map
planning ornamental grasses   casino adding topiary   parking in the back
steamrolling the yewed   dunes to   zero   waste resorts sending
rodents into the walls   like a purring   catapult   into the water
like   a   hole   in it   to   be   filled   in   mediately
millions of us flocking   to the coast swarming   every weekend
stuck in windshields   vipers prostrated   traffic   fending roadkill

Nothing like Thunder Bay—confounded Capital of Lost Cities   Mere   villages
outdo this one   This one escapes the imagination like it did the
rapidly capitalizing world   Like after *le lac supérieur* Like *big marsh* come
Grand Marais   A few log homes big, two churches deep, one mine
long, one commercial block lined in stolen limestone from an even older
ghost town down the coast   All which nature recaptured
in stunning color, with shocking resolution   Disappearance leaves a mark
A nick   of   Scandinavians   on the ear   of the wolf head lake
It started at the one   one-bench schoolhouse   Finnish pancake   breakfast
overrun with Norwegians from a rough August wreck   which   called for
harvesting all the blueberries from the one   one-bear-infested   bush
The bear the town mascot, pet and pest   swam off after the last of the
sturgeon never to be wrestled or rendered again   Then the lumber trades
And the shipping business   Then   everyone   just   took   the   train
Things vanish for obscenely practical reasons   You do it to yourself they
do it to you   you close your eyes   the globe spins   you finger
Land a fathom down the road and twice that in the lake   This one
was no different a beast   Never showed the whites of its eyes to anybody
Just clapped its shutters to go out   in an awe of resignation   one one-
forest-fire-sized   night   of the northern lights   Its   hide
exquisitely thick   Its jaw never shut

Free samples of cigarettes now that's the American spirit   so many
impoverished states of being   free and having choice   smoking at a
gas station   Indian Country smokes   we took a couple Sagos
my host bought a carton of Putters   I gifted him a lighter   now that's the
Canadian spirit   the province   of brotherly love   hanging smoggily over
other provinces of affiliation

We didn't have anything in common   theater
split ends   stretch marks   Pearl Jam
I'd rather be   with   an   animal
we were raced together   at the neck   two-headed brown
cowed   yet unceded   no man is   a reserve   and no one is
illegal   don't totally believe it   cuz I grew up bent   so hard   on being legal
but there were some at our Coptic church who came in through the back
door or the window   hard for some to grasp   Christians that are Arab
not that I believe   but   I can appreciate   embracing   the   country
through a window

He drove me all around   the   land   the bays   pulled the curtain on his
family   they laughed   the best Indian pizza   Debaj art centre   his
church   I still can't understand it   Catholic   Anishinaabe   the roofless
ruin by its side the site of a Crystal Shawanda country music video
and his troupe's plays and his   monologues   told me about a pack
of deer one morning swimming across the bay   bad fishing   turned   good
hunting   using   oars   to   knock   them   dead   rope around the heads
takes a long   slow   drag   gives me a taste   of his new song
all I remember is   *our half brothers   we half love you*   is all   I
needed to hear   a stranger in a strange land   is in a way home   I think
that Bible line oughta go

Yes I am a native   Arab   American   I welcome these indigenous
cats   all French dogs and British pigs and all   off-color   offspring   to   this
special place of   eternal   circling   that   I claim as my territory and I
place this   claim right   in with   everyone   else's   offensive   I hand over

fist feed my left foot   to   my   own   big   mouth   to   call   this   transience

settlement   I'm not proud   I accept all food and beverages and medicine

fresh and sweet   grass and water   sage and cedar sacred   and   cheap

tobacco   he gifted me   when I left and I put the box in the

dashboard   and went back looking for the 200-count unbranded you get

zipped in a plastic bag

Buying gas by lots   of grass   shooting animals   with their stuffing out
it's starving out   only the soil's rich and everybody's buying   local
Faygo   Black Bottom's up   for new urban renewal   the river's hot
the French is back   *rivière de* riot   lapping through the suburbs in Erie
quiet   I'm afraid

of what I'll do to you   if I moved here   the Tigers I'd let
lose   the bridges I'd burn with the houses I'd buy   urbane   farms   like
snakes   in fields of green   glass   bite us in the ass
invading hoods as saving them   finding purchase with the ease
of beads for islands   of pictures   on the verge of snapping

Balding campground on the "Sunrise Coast" and
who wants sunrise on hard-earned vacation

The sun going *BLAM* all day   no more composure   what an example
who can you look to   blue jay *CRACK* like an ax thrown up into a spruce
never to be seen again   but erupts   later on a trip to the showers
diving head-down into your dome   then back   never   to   be
seen   again   the stars go *POOF*   into the night   where   they're
supposed to live   off the grid   watch out for the bear   trap watch for
the belt   buckle raining down going *LOL GOTCHA* and the campfire casting
big doubts on all that seems benign   nature going *DON'T LOOK AT ME I
DIDN'T DO THIS TO US I CAN'T HELP YOU I'M NOT EVEN REMOTELY ON
THIS PLANET* not for you at least   out of chocolate   no harmonica   family of
raccoons *FAN OUT CHICKENSHITS*   falling out like a night burrito
into the tent sites   trying their hand with the fire-poking stick with
Huron flooding   folding   like waterbeds   'n' stuff in the strip mall park-
side going *MEGA MEGA SALE SALE* six-pack of whoopee cushions some lube and a
vape pen *THIS IS GLAMPING KIDS* goes the mom in the pop-up by the Porta-
Johns   you can never be safe   careful   too
because there's a dump   to be had anywhere people   this region is trash
the sky is trash   and it all burns pretty   well   till *BLAM*

51

Talks at Great Lakes Science Center; SS Meteor
Maritime Museum; Marine Museum of the Great Lakes;
Great Lakes Lore Maritime Museum; Great Lakes
Historical Society; Shipwreck . . .

Fish advisories, hatcheries, carbon and credit dioxide and card deals; oxygen depletion, leachate, oxen, chicken, scat, smelt, and eaten

Research, veto, funding dung, zoo- and phytoplankton, finding purchase, zebra mussel, alewife, sea lamprey, purple loosestrife, European buckthorn, exotic species, that is, immigration

Beautification, and eutrophication, lake stratification and turnover from the peopled epilimnion to the deep sunk hypo needling the tepid thermocline

Moisture-bearing care packages, hydrologic unicycles, suspended particles, and articles—the—Great Lakes, or a—they're one

When the early Lake Algonquin poured out three ways to the Atlantic and one way to the Mexico gulf, our region evolved as the first rest area in an era humanless

Land was cut into water by a constant stream of glaciers summering in pre-Georgian Bay; perverse creatures of the lust to wander camped their proto-RVs in fields of Pleistocene weeds; minerals were compacted to bracelets chains of islands big

"Civilization" was the frontier to nature; it sprung up everywhere, with its vistas, the love of which was only survival for us newbies with balls of eyes; pre-Americans vying with no British for ascendancy of Frenchless and non-Native-held lands—not even algae was invasive

But it was nonetheless languorous chaos in the wilderness—skin did grow thick on the teeth, and by it, time stoically passed

Language was impossible; vowels confused with consonants—water and
continent were one—consonants, and continents; with water, and vowels—

Everywhere was a sort of water-Pangaea, a lake somehow floating
invisibly in a sea—two Pangaeas; impossible   like your eyes, say
                                                    Two Pangaeas
                        deafening blue, jagged green flake at heart, black iris
                                    folding out the dark; first life
                                                    life is too, too
                                                    impossible
                            a touch away from your face and it's
                            as if I get a look at life from space
                            you see for yourself; see for me
                                    the world is two, two
                                    land and water
                                    shallow and possible
I wait and wade and wait and wade and wade and wait and wait and wade

Kneeling on Sarnia in the defunct scale model
fountain of the Great Lakes in Sarnia

Small heart of the Lakes, Lake St. Clair
an idea taking shape
from physical coastline
not like "The Heart of It All" Ohio
in the chest of the States
an idea stitched to shape
with a couple geopolitical lines

How many hearts can a place have
look at this model—there are so many centers
where families ply, lovers don't
where they go, the solitary stay away
and there are only so many places
where dogs are allowed
a couple countries, many nations
a province or two—Quebec, eight states
regions in region, Arrowhead, North Shore, Sunrise Coast, thumb
lower, upper, Leelanau, Keweenaw
peninsulas, Door, many others
One and only Manitoulin Island, Isle Royale, Apostle Islands—
the Thousand Islands, Thirty Thousand Islands, a handful more
Georgian Bay, the 6th Great Lake, or Lake Champlain
and Nipissing, Nipigon, Simcoe, St. Clair, 7ths
and each Lake

How many things is water
how big a thing
can one feel something real for
enough to really put their mind's
arms around it feel the heart kick
back, away
asking to be seen whole, broke
two halves folded to a near close
at the St. Clair River, Detroit River, St. Marys,

Straits of Mackinac, Niagara, and St. Lawrence
forgot all the rivers, channels, falls
streams and capillaries
it's infinite hearts
with just five chambers
it's only one thing
and it's the size of anything
you can ride
stretch wide to nearly splitting

With the lake engulfing the balcony
on the 41st floor

What's out there is fish and water fish and smaller
no delusions of being taken by some
body giant or self
possessed it's all science
there can't be monsters
for us to hang on
through the turbulence
and drag us under
where it's deathly quiet
it was just a sturgeon
in the depths of Michigan
or a bloated body lobbed up on your suit
surfing Chicago
got to be logical
there can't be monsters any more
than aliens
it's just science
that is a placeholder
to embody the fathomless
wish
there was a Lakes monster
so big it wouldn't have skin
but a surface
troughed and undryable
only its back visible
and its many pits dark
sockets and holes would have
to be an eye in some
hairs that clog the shore
it wouldn't have scales
it doesn't belong
in water either it's a monster
emerged near the outer harbor   retaining   water   like   a   bilge
tracking nets pants camo tans and teals shirt riptide chest sacky   milky

pool of wrinkles like a bib and a spare tire rolled off its waist to shore   it's
a creature not a monster sweetheart   scouring downtowns for a place to stay
recycling bays   of condos   grill shed on the roof deck   don't worry nothing
out there can hurt you   it can take care of itself   nothing out there but the
cold the open

As far as the Chicago Sanitary and Ship Canal
and no farther cuz watershed end

Now we can finally eat   the enemy with lemon vinegar and boiling oil
not like with extremists or corporations   the   I hate to say
for exotification   Asian   carp invading the Lakes   I hate to say it
from tributaries stuffed to guts with fish piss   poor in diversity   white rural
catfish sucking rock bottom while the Bighead Grass Silver Black take their
notorious leaps pulling themselves up by the gill-straps through glassy ceiling
to slap you in the dinghy face   like a school   of dueling gloves
sharp enough to de/recolonize   rich with abandon fish   and protein and roe
upward   each of millions   in the Chicago River   all kinds of carp in there
binding watersheds together   backward   unwholesome
industrious and immigrant   as the city's twentieth-century engineers
who perverted the course of nature   by throttling a river in reverse
through a continental divide   and let the fish   fly   so into the frying pan
Chicago   Milwaukee Green Bay   you already down it all   Cleveland
Buffalo Rochester I know you   hungry protect your borders and gorge
Ontario   get out your tartar sauce and panko   Michigan   you'll   be
surrounded   do the patriotic thing and eat   if they just change
their name to something more appetizing   something-something whitefish
a new shade of salmon   we're sold   we'd fight for our country
with gluttony   that's why we brought them here   that's why they survived

58

Geneva State Park no sight of the lake,
Geneva-on-the-Lake, OH

Last night we snuck into the state   park real late to sleep   in my
tent   by the car   on the paved driveway of a muddy site   drizzle invisible
in a wood pervasive with knocked-out Buckeyes   corn-fed and golden-haired
in the fires put out   a thick gauze sat   whispering   undocumented
we gulped each   half an orange watermelon   two itinerant sore
thumbs   stuck out   in the wooded preserve among cornstalks
we feasted on watermelon   as a family   for dinner with feta   pita
diet coke   last night we stole a night in our home state state park
but didn't go down to mom and dad's didn't see the Cleveland relatives Browns
Indians games mounds grandma's grave   last night it rained rain rained
and nothing heard   the lake stir once from the downpour   the morning
was   too   quiet   black and slick   we split for a diner
then   always novel to us   before any sighting in the woods of us
lights head low with the sun soon too to clean   its   plate
in the vapor of our gross great   lake Us   the vapor that's our family

59

Is it all rain and huddles there too   people all cheersing under awnings
you're all *I'm wearing a toque*   I'm all out of step   shooting hoops in the
showers   *boooooo* the water brims   splashing the shot off the rim
I wanna take a swim to you but the water stays here   wherever   in
the sewer aquifers another sphere   Can't be taken with

Ouch a conifer stings   of where you're from   these milk thistles, of where
you would be if you were with me still   fold a thing, lick the seam till it's
bled through, tear in two; no give   ready for the scrap-
book crafting   clouds split after rain   rivers and
lakes are licked ready for the rafting   try and take a part—no give
the heart wants what it—what water won't   love can't be taken with
the   water   stays   here
No, can't

The water stays here the steelhead mouths and bangs on the foam with its
good eye on a Buffalo intake station gulping what is Lake Erie now   next
Ontario St. Lawrence Atlantic   water   changing   name   midstream
*why can't I   why name me Lover   instead of The One Who Lives
how did they know   or did they doom me*
its gums' hook-holes whistling and fin up in punctuation   gills   heaving
dramatically   probing the air for a deep   breath of water   then gone
on to Niagara Falls—can't be taken   Won't stay

It's the basins that remain   with their decommissioned locks, pipelines, wrecks
of perishabilia   we step in every day, trying   at least once for that
mythical same river   We want it   more more   We can't   be swift enough

Bay City Street-View which now shows the
building demolished and the river yet bluer

You find the story, years old   Sears closing, testimonials
of selling shoes and dressing window fronts   post-idly   Street-Viewing
Bay City, MI   A weathered mural on its east wall   says Redwood, MN
So remote   its birthplace   Says that   below   a quaint
locomotive on a bit of track   Barrels rendered against a lone brick building
fading in a square   in a square   on the lone brick building

What an odd tribute for   noplace   local in   noplace local
You don't remember it in real life   Been through Bay City how many times
No good reason see the little largest city on Huron—on both sides of the border
What with the shipbuilding war-proud storied years   A locals'
sort of point of fact, to know   As if you were from here   watched the
freighters on the Saginaw   from a Salvation Army   stroller maybe Or during
the off-loading of a grocery cart   in first new winter American clothes
full of pins and bizarrely unworn   To last you clear
Off-street parking for five hundred cars   to OH or wherever
before they moved   the store out to the mall
1990 to be exact   You can pace virtually the whole derelict lot now
Scroll   along the river   on an unspecified day August 2012   say one o'clock
judging by the shadows   of Augusts   Maybe your birthday
Found yourself here for one a few years back   completely incidental and a
bit alone   Maybe you   were   born   to   be   from   Bay   City

The trolling ends there   past a shoddy gazebo   at a stiff piqued local man
and his tall hunched twin   Forever caught catching   nothing   at   the
riverfront without a Sears   Two slack rods each and you could've never
manned a one of them   Learned a trade   Worked a counter   Settled down
for thirty years wherever you'd have moved   Not your lot to make a
life   for a living   Next

Dark scribble County Line Rd that
breaks peninsula and mainland

Going down fast   but I'm there   here   caught in the light cut
you get to see   at best   one more time after the first impression   so take it in

Big beech leaf approach   porch swung   acreage blowing its till—not
the wind—me   speeding into the sun   funneled in the ridge

Before the recall takes effect   the overheating, powerless   steering, cruise
helplessness, wipers fly   off in the rain   the dark thrushes in
through the   selfsame crack in   the selfsame beeches

Sight   the opposite of floods—   floats   hardens   sinks

Collapsed into the east shore duneland   Immanently   Domain of the
national parks now   Or swallowed into Milwaukee possibly or into the Calumet
swampland   where Chicago fed   on the westbound   till the wheels
came off   Or still right up there in the UP somewhere   missing
mailboxes   a few garages   selling pasties   avoiding taxes
infrastructure skeletal in the algae   Not lost—   dead   Or no need found—
many more would be founded   An auguring fate   sort of   all-American
Like this lake itself   And the lake that swallows it Becomes it   A spirit of the
law   Haunting the Lakes   The continent

Lighthouse lit dawn opaque from
Marinette to Menominee

You can hide a lot in fog   I saw no terrace with chairs hot tub   outdoor
shower   Ski-Doo in silty lawn and beagle   dragging a bikini top behind after
sleeping in it   I was packing the car at dawn   all life seemed out of touch
of water   and its problems—a lot in fog   no sign but scent
of the smoked trout, no breakfast   no idea how to flop back into place
swim to   life and drive   to death   before the cape burns off
and leaves the world   again   to painfully
obvious warming   by then the neighborhood will have emptied onto the
beach till the beach fills in the neighborhood   how can things be always too
late?   always on the lookout for more ice   and   gas   the
climate changes right before you   know it a hundred years from
today, the moment   of efficacy as if it's always already passed   and all
that's left to do is lie and bask and look out—a gigantic tanker   slowly
shredding the horizon—a   lot in fog

Hangover dream I read every plaque and statue;
no business in Sault Ste. Marie

Today it's "voyager"   foggy out   wolfing white   doughnuts and creamer at
an Indian-Canadian motel lobby till check out   of life / the shoreline / time
always just enough to squander   map the long wrong way put your back into
the view   watch the road and mind one's own   "journey"   is   a
humiliating word   to spirit off; to mean to; to have so much extra-
vagance—who pulls up their roots and runs   like punking your alders while
they're in the bathroom come whipping out and tripping   bark stripped on
their naked shame and yelling out   your   special   name—your   species'
You son of a birch you who is that   native   not invasive   deciduous
who is forager   loiterer   stranger than me   settling the margins of leisure
Today it's Voyageurs   National Park is all   it was a freeway is all—money
in trees no cap   on the beaver   you met at dawn   in   no-time
when fog was   drunk to work   in waves of nausea and singing   alternately
the portages were a bitch   the cakewalk was the evening stretch
the pipe and cards and fire   water in their ears   the jerky   the friendly
natives   intoxicating   them   patronizing you   the   mixed-breed
quarter horse French quarter quarter Cree   quarter   tree   running   roots
along the water-highway   Today it's maritime museum   if it rains
If it's clear it's hunting   for a place to fade into locals   Today not
"voyager" it's tourist   loser   lover   of all

Drinks at Great Lakes WATER Institute; Great Lakes Brewing
Company; Great Lakes and St. Lawrence Governors and
Premiers; Alliance for the Great Lakes; Great Lakes Fishery
Commission; Great Lakes Protection Fund; Great . . .

Today there is a crisis of identity Today lines are drawn in water
Tonight there will be drinking and grinding This morning there was smog and
spunk This afternoon there are clouds, emails, egg salad This evening there will
be art and nature There will be more salads Women and men will civilize you,
then leave you like a sausage in the chain of violence, raw and mild as very
wilderness That is Today Let us, let me, see, show you

Earth has been the color green since circa about ~20,052,005 BC when
the Garden of Eden was not yet fabled but real God did the world Eve did Adam
God did in paradise Adam did Eve In Pangaea nothing was local; all was
globalized, flora and food turned on their head—you had your birds-of-paradise
and your Asian carp with your buttercups and trout; now that's a rosy meal and
no red herring, eh? If you thought Canada was natural, well, watch eowt

Mother Nature died when people went nuts in the summer of '69 in a
blaze—there are many shows about it—of glory The Cuyahoga caught fire
A phoenix was burnt Lake Erie took off "The environment" was born
as a subject for artists Phoenixes then expired Bigfoots were captured in New
Zealand and sired Bambi went to Blu-ray then cryogenically retired Finally we
struck oil in Iraq and fracked Old Faithful There are many studies about it
Many myths, many careers, disasters, many jokes, yr mama   is so   fat
                                                                          how fat
                                                                        she is
                                                       at first the earth was flat
                                                              then they buried
                                                                    yr mama
                                                                      so poor
                                                          so foolish, so fucked
                                                                    so old and
                                                     hot it's not even funny

66

Skyline Pkwy with vantage on the frozen
spit of Duluth and Superior

"The lake" is alive but the Lakes are dead
Now they can be rendered more vividly instead

These landscapes were painted by Mother Nature
They go for twenty-plus thousand bucks an acre

Horses are up a couple K a head
Now that they're useless they're more sacred

which is romantic enough
I came to paraphrase

not to memorize
a couple shades of blue

is all you really need
to know blue

Lake pray, 5 hr Isle Royale return ferry

Oh to reach one's destination before exhaustion

Navigate while gazing backward at a vista

Play the horn of one's choice at first touch

Sing a whole song through

without having to memorize it

To be the one the world speaks for

without first having to be endangered

I am the recycling and the garbage

One has no limits and no freedoms

You have the fire that burns the reigns

I am the stray you took to the valley

You are a shining night of trombones

One has a voice without a language

One is an animal not a vegetable

I don't have roots

I have no soul

I am The One Who Loves

You are The One Who Lives

You are the heartburn and the Milky Way

Neutralize one

Bind me to my senses

Show yourself in the flash in a window of a camera

Blind me to my selfies

One is not long enough for this world

Life is two handfuls borne to everyplace

I post my constellation over the dark choppy passage

I call for delivery tonight

Site said *small site dirt ground poor shade pond view one neighbour* what else could you do you booked it

Corolla tail caked and backed up close like an ass under a holey canopy Jesus but it's gorgeous the trinity of a pine and an oak and a birch with one crêpe branch split at the height of its beauty for picnic bench supports and bark to burn against hordes of zombie mosquitoes that ate up the special triple-XL citronella early in the week good thing grandma's dead good thing the family isn't here good thing the girlfriend good there's no kid you can't provide for anyone anything really but the off-red steed gas and the dear reader reading

Crossword dream again and the word was *sex* and you still didn't get it forgetting the rain fly and waking up nuts and cone bouncing between limb and trunk the tent gone dewy and see-through to where you can visualize the vast curvy ribbon unfurled all summer skirt the water temperature ecstatic and dad's cooler making cream of farmers' heirlooms with a big helping of ham-fisted sun and every map in reach regurgitating Huron to feed your voyeuristic trips like the great blue heron to peeping chicks

Left the world as is / ducked beneath the bridge / a curtain of cold rain / singing Kurt Cobain, yeah / Something in the way, yeah / an Army-green tarp waved / Something in the way / the fence was bent way back / Though they don't have any feeling

There's something in the way / Something in the park, yeah / There's something in the way / In the way of the park, yeah

Plenty places to live / if you take the world as is / It's okay to say good-bye / the homeless man is home / but not for that much longer / Now the geese are gone / the cranes keep coming back / that hide out when it rains / Though they don't have any feeling

There's something in the way / Something in the park, yeah / There's something in the way / In the way of the park, yeah

Love the world as is / though it won't feel nothing back / There's something in the park, yeah / Something about the park / Something in the park don't have any feeling

Great Black Swamp come heavy-use wetlands;
powers of Toledo origin song

Who let this wetland wet / Who cut this little inlet / Laid the hill for golden
hours / Fit the logs with the salamanders / Foretold the lichen and the mosses
/ Who offered the wildlife crossing

Along this promenade I sing / about how the world's made / my behorned
serenade to nobody but

Who wet this aggregate / Who raised this bamboo deck / Who had these
grasses mown / Who made the birches grow in groves / Who made this prairie
xeric / Carved out a space for heron

This is my behorned little dirge / I sing along this little bridge / about how this
little world's birthed by no body but

Who left this river wet / Sowed the embankment / Set the grade for the slope
of the island / Spawned the minnows to feed the walleye / Who knows the
ripples till flood / Who reads the dried-out flats of mud

About how the world's mocked up / I sing along this ply boardwalk / This is
where the trombones stop

for nobody / By no body but / you local / No melody but vocals / As is / La la /
La li / La las / La lis / As is

From the Flats to Edgewater
with GPS and her [illegible]

Driving through the warehouses it's like driving through a valley   as loosed as
we'd ever get   private   land   public   it's   all no man's
When we have to go around the train   standing   like   a   herd   of   beef
chewing and smoking and spitting   we go to the overpass   to get to
Edgewater   two over   the outta true tracks
then the snaked Cuyahoga   a deer trail between them and the
manufacturing blazed out to drinking spot

Back down we can't see much of anything   a couple blue licks through vines
of fencing   the river thickening   by the road crawling in
the opposite direction   useless   taking this route   long   meandering   course
of least resistance cemented into the hip Flats fresh with sidewalks and a-
bridged to a point of incomprehension   development   just   ahead
of the curve

The crossing always clears   eventually   if we can just idle
between the goods and   debris   the bucks and the beach
we'll get to the piers eventually   get spit out there   turn back on their city
take in the compromise   we've   come   a   long   way
they tell us   we can go anywhere   they let us

Up where the basin hooks hard: here lies Keweenaw   Lake Superior buried here
Miles of mines down   and out   of trains   wrest   in pieces in
dusky mountains of copper tailing   dusty mansion and cathedral
brick   You get a little taste of the place just by
standing in the wind

Calumet: when a town goes boom   heritage   the ensuing cloud
ever up in the air   Houghton and Hancock: forever one another's
mine and canary   for good or ill   Eagle: nestled and hammered over by Copper
Harbors both of mostly ossified fiber of the moral variety

You get to know people just by standing around in their joints   Up here
the buildings have good bones—   worked to   Sticking   out   on
the scenic drives   the Keweenaw wreck dives in the shallows grave
Good bones   if you're speculating   homes for
the weekend   You barely start to get to know the character of a place bye

We went to the Elk Rapids beach to finish our fish and cooler   a soccer sort
of volleyball there, grandmas babysitting   to find an open bathroom
we waded across a little channel   marina   yachts   blonds in clogs
crossing the channel against us   to the public side   matching Petoskey stone
necklaces around their burnt red Adam's apples

The marina's bathrooms were private   a bunker   with a glass lobby and
keycard entry   two more boys came backing out   preening their reflections
in perfectly fit lederhosen   all four vying for a last laugh
we clung to the berm   on   to a public building   no sidewalk   over a bridge
over water wrinkled   and dark   garbage bag   this bathroom had no
windows no doors on the stalls   we went   peed next to each other
flaky gray cinder blocks inches from   our noses   we couldn't get the fish
off our hands

Crossing back through the marina lot we saw more boats drove in   coasting on
waxed dollies   masts stiff above other boats and cars   a predation
of the lot and Lake Michigan beyond   we stopped   a   moment
midchannel   the setting   sky   was outrageous harmony   on the bay
eating up the whole east arm   these Black girls   with tattoos   tucked
in huge white shirts   on our side   fought with laughter in the shallows

Past Prescott's where I cross graft   the border   to   the   bridge   to
Ogdensburg   scar   wrap   the   St.   Lawrence   in   white   flags   ice   sheets   it'll
heal it'll grow   I make it over   easily no one knows who's the host who's
the implant   over here—right over   fluids have been traded
illicitly for over two hundred years   two prohibitions wars towers a new
York plunged into   fighting   its kin in Canada   over a sliver of moon
shine   casks   caskets   lobsterbacks   drowned Black runaways rusty
rightfully Haudenosaunee muskets   at the fort   a fish got sick   in a pale
seaway of algae when I peered in to touch and   I revulsed in sympathy with
the Lakes? have come to this   a bottleneck of some 1,800 islands some
counting   some policing   the trashed   the privatized   the preserved   the
proud the militarized the few   that hold their brush and flood and hide
tearing down the dotted line   so no one else can sign and settle
so many have forged on already   a restless Americanesse
on   a   split   porch   composing   Mad   Libs   on   a   beverage-heavy
breakfast tray   mouth bit   in cursive   wheelchair missing spokes kids
attacking the front yard from the back   behind   which   Canada   drinks
what's a river now   here's Nick's Liquor now   across   the   mile   divide
I can see the Prescott LCBO the Liquor Control Board of Ontario's   no
colourful sea   between us   no favoured lexicon—a long   wet   blank
she cursed the pen and threw it   they squirt
their guns   and the U.S. drinks in kind

Struck on Flowerpot how close I was to
having gotten us citizenship

A boat begs to us nose wet on the sheer   tableaucloth   flecked with gulls
and look at that sky   just torn to shreds   I'll be back   with my wallet
someday   let's go   home   together have the cookout in a yard
let's turn this thing around   get pregnant for   Canada   Day
is about dreaming big in small places   Big Bay   Capital of Stone
—skipping   what else   says kids but
this   Flowerpot Island

Formations that seem too good   to be true   to last   climbed up and
yep capped in concrete   then a stack crashed on the grill   and me too
and the planner that caught fire you doused clean   of all figures in
a cold shower   of Sleeman beer   ha got me   too   good   to
be true   I know we'd said we could afford a boat
without a sail inboard'll do   afford some land if it's north enough
barren enough   a rocky island   here's thousands
in forgotten Huron   it better   cracked   we   glitter glue

77

                        Between Penetanguishene and Parry Sound
Erie and   Buffalo   Espanola   to the Soo   Ste. Marie
or St. Ignace through Escanaba all the way   to Packers stadium I hardly
recall   that weary leg with the pedal held   back to Toronto at the end
to do the word problems I've been at for years now   takes years   to reckon
the gap   where cities flood   the rivers that pull them out to stud
the Lakes at night like hoary constellations hooked to hills   I don't wanna
just write maps   I   don't   wanna   just   capitalize   the   stars
highlighted out from all the dim-lit passes   what about the littler bays
in Green Bay   points off Point Pelee   the   rehabbed   lakefronts
bypassed by force of the rich enlightened masses   what about the gridless
islands they practice on in their cursive-named yachts   I forgot and saw
Neebish   Little Kitchener   Michipicoten   Bois Blanc   Sugar
Island   the   half   million   little   riddled   docks   that   hang   like   cigarettes
pushing   writers not to quit   but   draw

Staircase down to a high overlook wrapped in trees

Take a picture   before   things   get   too   beautiful   because
they will get beautiful   oh yes   and you don't wanna miss that
do you   in person   lean in   stay   close   stay   tame
be human   don't forget to quit   don't forget to drop everything
in the water   don't forget your allergies in spring   humility   bless you
don't forget to litter with nature in autumn   solidarity   leaves-in-arms
in   communing   with   nature   you   can   say   a   few words   in
gibberish   stay wild   stay true   stay sweet   stay still   don't change
don't go don't stop loon   please bear   with me

Pukaskwa vision of winters here
when tent blew into lake

Out of the   blue   come the whitecaps   moaning
with ice on their teeth   spawn
on the back of a titanic mom   tail curled   to breaking   over their soft
translucent pricks   to save them all   consume the one

Cheated lake   cold-blooded caregiver   just try and take me   keep me
alive long enough to poison you   with my pyscho activity   geography
hustling like I'm one of yours   but you got none

Wipe us out   crash the ice shelves from the shore cliffs   from cottages the
solar panels   rend the light   from house   where you breach with a wave
of your hand   wind   wand   of your claw   you cannibalize with
consume yourself   to save   us all

Big Bay de Noc bluff which resuscitated
wonder so late on

Here again happy thing my size a love for me I come and grift whenever I'm in a
100-mile radius   then minutes up a bluff walk   I'm   back to
respire in the decay   my little coiled tree chimera   what are we   what
have we done   knots undone to chalky contours all twisted and cleft
and leaping for joy in my eyes   with ants in its eyes   two little lizard limbs
the sun forced back   to life a little while longer with its light
for alms poor thing no fingers no palms no spine   in the paper-thing
emulchiated trunk that holds the whole cliff out to tango where other nearby
crests have fallen   in   love with the piercing bay below alive with rockslide
the tree-line aquarium   the cardinals perch   why can't they be   what can we

I'm a mottled slug at heart with heart like any beast no sense of how I look how
gawkily smoothly smeared in place   I bend over backward too to feel
the clouds on my face the wind lapping at my sappy heel I swab the earth
with my eye stalk   with   I'll never leave you alone my love my that
obscure figure of nature   like a lie   in wait   when I come to
anthropomorphize the dead and living   we'll always be so close this far
arm's length enough for a good throw   project on   wilderness bodies
creatures spirit   me either   leaning into the void signaling
a caterpillar   steps out of the needles onto the trail maybe also feeling a
texture change too big to sustain

To Marquette after Pictured Rocks, feeling
destined/not that way

But, moving on   achingly so   parting birds   keeping the peace, distance
spellbound to a chain of vistas   turning inward, inland now   Canada clouds
America storms   a line slashed in the waves way out
sunk for all we know   border   so long   parting words
disturbing the peace, balance   a fray of gulls, a spray of crackers
a mouth of logs, a foot in history   a page of ice, a washed-out memo in
the margins   lines in sand   parsing words
                                staying on
                            accepting the peace,
                                challenge

I've hit bottom, friends
rock
to you
your Mediterranean
interred sea
where I am from
These are my dad's trunks
These are my dad's calves
These are my dad's chests
These are my dad's hands
This blood, my dad's—the sharks would come
but there are no sharks here
where am I from
folks; we from
there's no predators here
save storms
and waves
of immigration
but all over the Lakes
are shaped like predators
seething wolf leering shark
mouths' points
shipwrecks stand
a better chance of a homecoming
than the packs of immigrants that beached
at drowned wolf blinded shark
tongues warped into
Wendat and English
naming maiming
limbs of peninsulas
ripshod creatures' claims for places
that no one wants
stuck together families like amphibious gangs
growing back parts

And the world, entire
would load
before your eyes

And there's no more
And caches clear and all songs stream at once
The sound delayed, avatars retired

And all seasons complete at once
with the earth tilted on its axis no more
The weekend's lightning, languorous

arms stretched after lunch—you can't take more
And the robes are soaked; why,
they can't absorb another drop

and what's more
washes over unimpeded now
And there's more

The morning after
all justice meted out
all grudges would be lost

in the cloud
And power would go out
And all leisure would be more

radical then
And the fight would go out of you
with the world at your fingertips

guiding your hand
to the ends of luxury
It doesn't get any better than this

there's more
of the same
And who could want more

Coming into one Killarney out of another more wild
(and what could that mean from here on)

Killarney park was lakes made of mountain; wild   this fringe town
Killarney is the pool shed of mountains, so wild   canoes   on
bikes, outboard blowout sale, leaf bag of maple   leaf flags   and me,
returning from the backcountry in a poncho like a tent on foot   like a
bone-wet bobcat on all twos   sneaking into town to eat and fitting right in so
wild   I saw a big black bear right up my path, when I hiked into
La Cloche   from then on: strangling cowardice and never
can let go—it would flame up instantly, reinflate   I sang for two days
straight at the spook of that bear   those mountains   I was in—
fearsome white quartzite cliffs choked in firs and birches hanging like wreaths
in teeth   it was So Utterly Wild and   beautiful   fortunate to scare
and sing   yet   in all that splendor   I'd suddenly desired the
highway side-lands   the cattails with the pop cans   in a creek, not
pristine, juxtaposed to the road and drafts of cars   the contaminated
scene   the lake's edge was utterly clear where I camped depth changing
with each wane of the sun in cloud   inside, waterlogged black branches of
rejected trees logged maybe in the 1800s mazed from moment to next
pocked by rocks and milfoil fazes like looking into the sun   looking   down
and seeing eclipses in your reflection   and wind would come from far, mesh
the treetops loud briefly then whoosh around the bend   I thought of
cars between mart stops   on byways, buying flip-flops and groceries in
one swoop, old people toting grandkids, taking curves with   rare   instinct
from far before the first caution sign and crashing on with red taillights
around side rails as if caught in a pendulum   then swinging free with a
weee   we who   whew   my body was as if dredged inclined to make of
those ripples familiar hundreds of shortcut car arcs   and forget the animals
the bear   I was freaked of   the authorities so quick deferred to   the same
difference   come on   boss   give chase   through the stoplights
to one of your favorite dumpsters   the   wildest
blue yonder's no sky sea whatever, water   but just the frontier, the edge of,
where worlds knock like bumpers with the weary driver waking to backseat
squeals about a tall turkey or portly porcupine seen marching out of the trees
how bad could it be?,   coming out of the collapsing green, to just
patronize the lakeside   fish & sundae shack   with   some   backwoods
currency bit up good to prove it's real

Acknowledgments

This work was kept alive across far-flung years with the influence and care of Kathryn and Henry; Nasrat and Mary and Amira and family; Josh Theroux; Emily Nilsen; Tom Comitta; M. L. Martin; Rhett McNeil; Chris Fischbach; Molly Van Avery; Shane Darwent; Rena Detrixhe; Tali Weinberg; Marion Gast; Charles Campbell; Sarah Peters; Emily Gastineau; Dave Marks; Matthew Million; James Irwin; Victoria Stanton; Mark Feddes; Rachel and the Elliotts; Fionncara MacEoin; Karen Solie; Tim Bowling; Tim Lilburn; Lana Barkawi; Angelique Power; Ruth Pszwaro; Joseph Osawabine; Mizna and the writing group; Coffee House Press; Tulsa Artist Fellowship; the Joyce Foundation; the Grand Marais Art Colony; Pillsbury House; Red Eye Theater; the Mississippi Watershed Management Organization; the Minnesota Museum of American Art; the Soap Factory; the Minnesota State Arts Board; the Provincetown Community Compact; Salem Art Works; Debajehmujig Creation Centre; Write On, Door County; Varuna; Crosshatch Center for Art & Ecology/ISLAND; Banff Centre for Arts and Creativity; the Theatre Centre; Montréal, Arts Interculturels; and dear but missed others and the dear places and spaces of the Great Lakes.

With recognition of the many enduring Native and First Nations peoples of the vast Great Lakes region, despite their dispossession and genocide—with recognition of Black communities enduring through enslavement and systemic racism which make North America what it is—with recognition of the xenophobia, sexism, classism, and other supremacist legacies to transcend—these nature poems were written.

LITERATURE
is not the same thing as
PUBLISHING

Coffee House Press began as a small letterpress operation in 1972 and has grown into an internationally renowned nonprofit publisher of literary fiction, essay, poetry, and other work that doesn't fit neatly into genre categories.

Coffee House is both a publisher and an arts organization. Through our *Books in Action* program and publications, we've become interdisciplinary collaborators and incubators for new work and audience experiences. Our vision for the future is one where a publisher is a catalyst and connector.

Funder Acknowledgments

Coffee House Press is an internationally renowned independent book publisher and arts nonprofit based in Minneapolis, MN; through its literary publications and *Books in Action* program, Coffee House acts as a catalyst and connector—between authors and readers, ideas and resources, creativity and community, inspiration and action.

Coffee House Press books are made possible through the generous support of grants and donations from corporations, state and federal grant programs, family foundations, and the many individuals who believe in the transformational power of literature. This activity is made possible by the voters of Minnesota through a Minnesota State Arts Board Operating Support grant, thanks to the legislative appropriation from the Arts and Cultural Heritage Fund. Coffee House also receives major operating support from the Amazon Literary Partnership, Jerome Foundation, McKnight Foundation, Target Foundation, and the National Endowment for the Arts (NEA). To find out more about how NEA grants impact individuals and communities, visit www.arts.gov.

Coffee House Press receives additional support from the Elmer L. & Eleanor J. Andersen Foundation; the David & Mary Anderson Family Foundation; Bookmobile; Dorsey & Whitney LLP; Foundation Technologies; Fredrikson & Byron, P.A.; the Fringe Foundation; Kenneth Koch Literary Estate; the Matching Grant Program Fund of the Minneapolis Foundation; Mr. Pancks' Fund in memory of Graham Kimpton; the Schwab Charitable Fund; Schwegman, Lundberg & Woessner, P.A.; the Silicon Valley Community Foundation; and the U.S. Bank Foundation.

The Publisher's Circle of Coffee House Press

Publisher's Circle members make significant contributions to Coffee House Press's annual giving campaign. Understanding that a strong financial base is necessary for the press to meet the challenges and opportunities that arise each year, this group plays a crucial part in the success of Coffee House's mission.

Recent Publisher's Circle members include many anonymous donors, Patricia A. Beithon, the E. Thomas Binger & Rebecca Rand Fund of the Minneapolis Foundation, Andrew Brantingham, Dave & Kelli Cloutier, Louise Copeland, Jane Dalrymple-Hollo & Stephen Parlato, Mary Ebert & Paul Stembler, Kaywin Feldman & Jim Lutz, Chris Fischbach & Katie Dublinski, Sally French, Jocelyn Hale & Glenn Miller, the Rehael Fund-Roger Hale/Nor Hall of the Minneapolis Foundation, Randy Hartten & Ron Lotz, Dylan Hicks & Nina Hale, William Hardacker, Randall Heath, Jeffrey Hom, Carl & Heidi Horsch, the Amy L. Hubbard & Geoffrey J. Kehoe Fund, Kenneth & Susan Kahn, Stephen & Isabel Keating, Julia Klein, the Kenneth Koch Literary Estate, Cinda Kornblum, Jennifer Kwon Dobbs & Stefan Liess, the Lambert Family Foundation, the Lenfestey Family Foundation, Joy Linsday Crow, Sarah Lutman & Rob Rudolph, the Carol & Aaron Mack Charitable Fund of the Minneapolis Foundation, George & Olga Mack, Joshua Mack & Ron Warren, Gillian McCain, Malcolm S. McDermid & Katie Windle, Mary & Malcolm McDermid, Sjur Midness & Briar Andresen, Daniel N. Smith III & Maureen Millea Smith, Peter Nelson & Jennifer Swenson, Enrique & Jennifer Olivarez, Alan Polsky, Robin Preble, Alexis Scott, Ruth Stricker Dayton, Jeffrey Sugerman & Sarah Schultz, Nan G. Swid, Kenneth Thorp in memory of Allan Kornblum & Rochelle Ratner, Patricia Tilton, Stu Wilson & Melissa Barker, Warren D. Woessner & Iris C. Freeman, and Margaret Wurtele.

For more information about the Publisher's Circle and other ways to support Coffee House Press books, authors, and activities, please visit www.coffeehousepress.org/pages/donate or contact us at info@coffeehousepress.org.

Moheb Soliman is an interdisciplinary poet from Egypt and the Midwest who has presented writing, performance, installation, and video projects at diverse literary, art, and public spaces around the U.S. and Canada. Moheb has received multiple national and regional grants and residencies and has degrees from the New School for Social Research and the University of Toronto. He lives in Minneapolis, Minnesota, where he was the program director for the Arab American literary journal and arts organization Mizna before receiving a three-year Tulsa Artist Fellowship award. Learn more at www.mohebsoliman.info.

HOMES was designed by Bookmobile
Design & Digital Publisher Services.
Text is set in Arno Pro.